# Carlsbad Cavern

by Moira Anderson

EDUCATORS PUBLISHING SERVICE
Cambridge and Toronto

Series Authors: Kay Kovalevs and Alison Dewsbury
Series Consultant: Melinda Rice
Commissioning Editors: Sarah Russell, Bonnie Lass, and Sethany Rancier Alongi
Senior Editorial Manager: Sheila Neylon
Text by Moira Anderson
Edited by Robyn O'Sullivan and Laura A. Woollett
Designed by Tanya De Silva
Photographic research by Dan Nicholls

Making Connections program developed by Educators Publishing Service, a division of School Specialty Publishing and by Harcourt Education, a division of Reed International Books Australia Pty Ltd



ISBN 0-8388-3320-9

2010 2009 2008 2007 2006
10 9 8 7 6 5 4 3 2 1

Printed in China

**Acknowledgments**

**Photographs**
The author and the publisher would like to thank the following for permission to reproduce the copyright material in this book.

Animals Animals, pp. 11, 12, 17, 23; Australian Picture Library/Corbis, cover pp. 3, 4, 20; Australian Picture Library/Minden Pictures, pp. 6, 14; Avesphoto.com/Mike Danzenbaker, p. 5 (right); Charles Mills, p. 16; Nature Picture Library, p. 5 (left); The Otter Side, p. 21; Photodisc, pp. 7 (right), 9, 15; Photolibrary, pp. 8, 10, 13, 19; Steve Metz Photography; p. 7 (left).

Every effort has been made to trace and acknowledge copyright. The author and publisher would welcome any information from people who believe they own copyright to material in this book.

# Introduction

Every year, thousands of people visit Carlsbad Cavern in New Mexico. Carlsbad Cavern is one of the world's largest caves. For part of the year, it is also home to more than one type of animal.

Visitors at Carlsbad Cavern

The inside of Carlsbad Cavern

Bats and birds don't normally live together. However, every summer, cave swallows and Mexican free-tailed bats make Carlsbad Cavern their home.

Mexican free-tailed bat

Cave swallow

The bats and birds have been sharing this home since 1966, when the first cave swallows arrived at Carlsbad Cavern. To know why this is unusual, we need to learn more about bats and birds.

# What Do Bats and Birds Look Like?

Bats have furry bodies with short legs and feet. Some bats have weak legs and don't use them to walk. But all bats use their legs and feet to hang from branches and rocks. Each foot has five toes and claws that help them to grip when they are hanging upside down.

A fruit bat hanging upside down to rest

Birds' bodies are covered with feathers. Like bats, they have legs and feet. Birds use them to walk or hop along. Most birds have only four toes with claws. Like bats, many birds have short legs. But birds that are fast runners or wade through water have long legs.

Birds can have long or short legs.

A bat in flight

Both bats and birds use wings to fly. Bats' wings are made of smooth skin stretched over their arms and fingers. Bats use their long fingers to hold out their wings when they are flying.

A bird in flight

Birds' wings are covered in feathers. Like bats, they have arm and finger bones. The bones are hollow so they are very light. But they are strong enough to hold the wings out for flying.

# Where Do Bats and Birds Live?

Bats live in dark places. Many live in large groups. They sleep during the day. When night falls, they go out to find food.

Bats hanging from rocks as they sleep

Most birds look for food during the day and sleep at night. They sleep together in large groups on tree branches, in bushes, or in holes. Birds use twigs, leaves, and grass to make nests for their young. They make their nests in bushes and trees, on the ground, or on ledges.

Birds sleeping on a tree branch

# Bat and Bird Families

Baby bats grow inside the mother's body. After they are born, they hang upside down like their mothers. Mother bats produce milk to feed their babies.

A baby bat using its toes and claws to hang upside down

Most birds lay eggs in nests. Baby birds grow inside the eggs. Birds use their body heat to keep their eggs warm. When the young have grown enough, they break out of the eggs.

Parents find juicy insects to feed the young birds. When the young birds have learned to fly and find their own food, they leave the nest.

A mother bird feeding her babies

# Finding Food

Most bats have sharp teeth for eating. They mainly eat insects, but some eat fruit, fish, and frogs.

Many bats use echolocation (say *EK-oh-low-KAY-shun*) to find food. They make high-pitched sounds. The sounds bounce off objects and make echoes. The bats follow the echoes, which lead them to their food.

A bat hunting an insect

Birds do not have teeth. They have a hard bill, or beak. Different birds eat different food such as insects, fish, fruit, meat, and seeds. Each kind of bird has a bill shape that best suits the kind of food it eats.

Birds with different beaks

# Carlsbad Cavern

There are so many differences between bats and birds, it is hard to imagine them living together. But that's just what happens in Carlsbad Cavern!

From early spring until October, about 350,000 Mexican free-tailed bats live in a passageway inside the cavern. About 2,000 cave swallows also arrive at the cavern in early spring. They live inside the entrance of the cavern.

A cave swallow in flight

Thousands of Mexican free-tailed bats in Carlsbad Cavern

The bats and birds come to Carlsbad Cavern to have their babies and raise them. Baby bats are born in the cavern. Here, they are safe from predators.

Each mother usually has only one baby bat a year. She gives birth while she is hanging onto the ceiling with her toes and thumbs. The new baby bat holds onto the ceiling or its mother.

A baby bat holding onto its mother

Cave swallows use mud, twigs, leaves, and feathers to make nests for their young on the walls of the cavern. They lay two to five eggs in their nests.

A cave swallow nest

The young birds are old enough to fly about three weeks after they hatch. Cave swallows return to Carlsbad Cavern each summer to lay eggs and raise their young.

Cave swallows picking up mud to make their nests

# Visiting Carlsbad Cavern

Thousands of people visit Carlsbad Cavern each year. They watch cave swallows diving around the entrance to the cavern during the day. After the sun goes down, people observe huge numbers of bats swarming out of the cavern.

Bats and birds have many differences. But Carlsbad Cavern is a special home where these animals can live together.

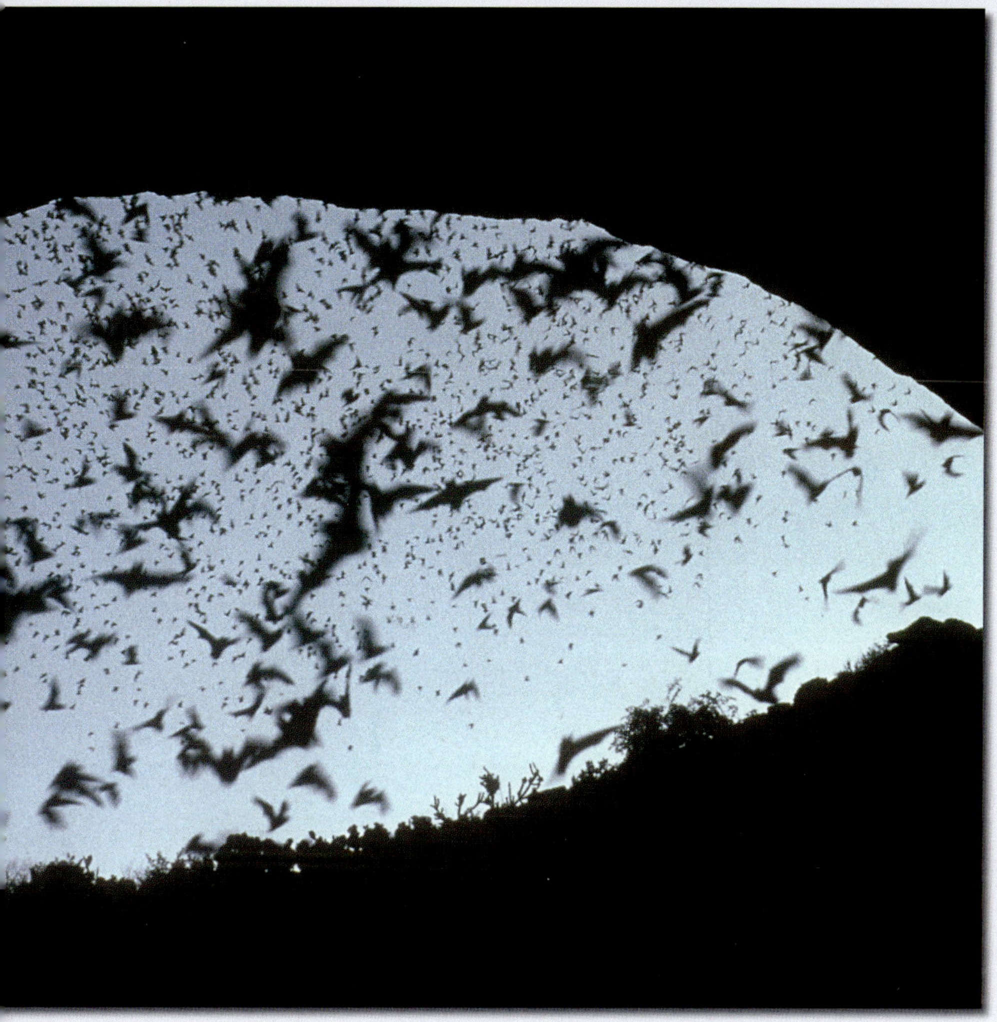

Bats swarming out through the cavern entrance to hunt for food

# Index